e Story of the Civi

REEDOM RIDES
in Photog

David Aretha

Enslow Publishers, Inc.
40 Industrial Road
Box 398
Berkeley Heights, NJ 07922
USA

http://www.enslow.com

Library of Congress Cataloging-in-Publication Data

Aretha, David.

    The story of the civil rights freedom rides in photographs / David Aretha.

      pages cm. — (The story of the Civil Rights Movement in photographs)

    Includes index.

    Summary: "Discusses the Freedom Rides, an important event in the Civil Rights Movement, including the riders who risked their lives, the violence the riders faced, and the successful integration of interstate buses and terminals"—Provided by publisher.

    ISBN 978-0-7660-4236-0

    1. Freedom Rides, 1961—Pictorial works—Juvenile literature. 2. African Americans—Civil rights—Southern States—History—20th century—Pictorial works—Juvenile literature. 3. African American civil rights workers—Southern States—History—20th century—Pictorial works—Juvenile literature. 4. Civil rights workers—Southern States—History—20th century—Pictorial works—Juvenile literature. 5. Southern States—Race relations—Pictorial works—Juvenile literature. I. Title.

    E185.61.A676 2014

    323.1196'073075—dc23

                           2012045749

Future editions:

Paperback ISBN: 978-1-4644-0415-3

Single-User PDF ISBN: 978-1-4646-1227-5

EPUB ISBN: 978-1-4645-1227-8

Multi-User PDF ISBN: 978-0-7660-5859-0

Printed in the United States of America

112013 Bang Printing, Brainerd, Minn.

10 9 8 7 6 5 4 3 2 1

To Our Readers: We have done our best to make sure all Internet Addresses in this book were active and appropriate when we went to press. However, the author and the publisher have no control over and assume no liability for the material available on those Internet sites or on other Web sites they may link to. Any comments or suggestions can be sent by e-mail to comments@enslow.com or to the address on the back cover.

Table of Contents

An African-American family in a "Negro Waiting Room" in Oklahoma City in 1955.

Introduction

It was a hot summer day in Mississippi, and young James Farmer, Jr., needed to quench his thirst. After peering through the screen door of a drugstore, he asked his mother if she could buy him a soda. She said she could not. When they got home, his mother told him the harsh truth: The store did not sell soda to black people. "My mother fell across the bed and cried," he said.

Throughout his life, Farmer fought against racism. In 1961, he became famous as a leader of the Freedom Rides. But fourteen years before that, he rode for justice in the Journey of Reconciliation.

Farmer and Bayard Rustin, leaders of the Congress of Racial Equality (CORE), began the Journey of Reconciliation. CORE members strove to end racial injustice in America. Even though slavery had been abolished in 1865, whites still oppressed African Americans up to the 1960s. This was especially true in the South.

Up until the 1960s, southern society was segregated. A segregated society means that the dominant racial group separates and mistreats a less-powerful group. Whites held all the leadership positions within the southern states. They created laws that benefited their race and were oppressive to black citizens. Blacks were forced to use segregated facilities, which were not just separate but inferior. African Americans were confined to "colored" restaurants, outhouses, churches, drinking fountains, pools, and the like. State governments provided far less funding for black schools. African-American students received a poor education.

In many places in the South, buses were segregated. Among the many segregation injustices on buses, whites sat in the front of the buses and black riders had to sit in the back. In 1946, the U.S. Supreme Court outlawed segregation on *interstate* busing. On an interstate bus ride, a bus travels from one state to another.

In April 1947, CORE members (black and white) tested this Supreme Court ruling. In the Journey of Reconciliation, they boarded buses from two companies— Greyhound and Trailways—and rode through the South. Black CORE riders sat in the front of the buses, and some shared seats with white CORE riders. Whites in the South responded angrily.

The Journey of Reconciliation received little national publicity. Back then, the mainstream media paid little attention to issues involving African Americans. However, their story appeared in newspapers that were published for black readers. The CORE riders' courageous efforts inspired many African Americans. The Journey was one of the first steps in the growing civil rights movement.

The movement began in earnest in 1955. That year, Rosa Parks refused to yield her seat to a white man on a segregated bus in Montgomery, Alabama. Reverend Martin Luther King, Jr., led a yearlong bus boycott by Montgomery's black citizens. Their success sparked other African Americans to action. Beginning in 1960, thousands of civil rights activists staged sit-ins. In a restaurant sit-in, for example, they sat in the whites-only section until they were served.

The 1961 Freedom Rides were sparked by a Supreme Court decision. In 1958, African-American college student Bruce Boynton rode a Trailways bus from Washington, D.C., to Montgomery, Alabama. During a stop at a Trailways bus terminal in Virginia, Boynton entered the terminal's restaurant. He sat in the white section of the restaurant and ordered a sandwich. When he was asked to move to the black section, he refused. He was arrested.

Boynton's lawyers appealed his case all the way to the U.S. Supreme Court. In December 1960, the Court sided with Boynton. The Court outlawed segregation in interstate *facilities*—not just the buses themselves. These facilities included bus terminals' restaurants, restrooms, and waiting rooms.

By 1961, James Farmer had become president of CORE. One day, Farmer was talking with staff members Gordon Carey and Tom Gaither about the Supreme Court's Boynton decision. They discussed how CORE should respond. Carey and Gaither talked about staging something like the Journey of Reconciliation. They wanted to call it the Freedom Rides. Farmer liked the idea. They talked about having CORE members, black and white, board buses and head to the South. This time, black passengers would enter whites-only restaurants, restrooms, and waiting rooms.

Farmer thought about riding the buses to the Deep South states, including Alabama and Mississippi. These states were especially dangerous. In the Deep South, segregationists (supporters of segregation) often reacted violently to civil rights activism.

But Farmer forged ahead with his brave plan. He said that CORE wanted to put "the movement on wheels . . . to cut across state lines and establish the position that we were entitled to act any place in the country, no matter where we hung our hat and called home, because it was our country."

CORE had been founded in 1942 on the principles of nonviolence. Founders had followed the example of Mohandas Gandhi and his followers. They had used nonviolent civil disobedience to help win independence for India from the British. The CORE riders would follow these principles. If attacked, they would not fight back. CORE members had been trained in nonviolent tactics. For example, they were taught the best way to protect their faces if punched or kicked.

The Freedom Rides would begin on May 4, 1961. That day, thirteen Freedom Riders—seven black and six white—would depart on two buses from Washington, D.C. The riders on one bus would be beaten with clubs, bottles, and metal pipes. The other bus would be bombed.

The rides for freedom would turn into a fight for survival.

Several CORE members look at a map of their Freedom Ride route. They include (left to right) Edward Blankenheim, James Farmer, Jr., Genevieve Hughes, Reverend B. Elton Cox, and Hank Thomas. The Freedom Rides began in Washington, D.C., and were supposed to end in New Orleans.

Chapter 1

Riding Into DANGER

Creating a Crisis

On May 4, 1961, the thirteen Freedom Riders boarded two buses, a Greyhound and a Trailways. Most Riders were members of CORE. Two were women and the rest were men. They were of various ages— from young to old. The Riders planned to ride through Virginia, North Carolina, South Carolina, Georgia, Alabama, Mississippi, and Louisiana. They would stop at bus terminals, where black members would use whites-only waiting rooms and restrooms. Whites would use the waiting rooms and restrooms designated for blacks. CORE leader James Farmer, Jr., expected the "racists of the South to create a crisis," as noted in the book *Voices of Freedom*. Farmer *hoped* that whites would attack Freedom Riders. If they did, he believed, Americans would demand an end to segregation.

Historically, segregation rules forced blacks in the South to sit in the rear of buses. On the two Freedom Ride buses, black CORE members sat in the front seats. They had the right to do so under federal law.

Risking Their Lives

From May 4 to 13, the Freedom Riders endured one violent attack. In Rock Hill, South Carolina, whites punched and kicked Riders Al Bigelow and John Lewis. The segregationists were angry because Lewis had tried to sit in a whites-only waiting room. On May 13, the Freedom Riders ate dinner with Martin Luther King, Jr., in Atlanta, Georgia. King warned that worse violence likely lay ahead. "You will never make it through Alabama," he said, as recalled in the book *Walking With the Wind.*

On May 14, segregationists firebombed the Greyhound Freedom Ride bus near Anniston, Alabama.

Attacked in Anniston

At 1 P.M. on May 14, the Greyhound bus pulled into Anniston, Alabama. The bus station was closed. No one seemed to be around. Suddenly, several dozen whites raced toward the bus. They carried clubs, chains, and metal pipes. They angrily smashed the windows and slashed the tires. Genevieve Hughes feared that she might be killed. As she recounted in Raymond Arsenault's *Freedom Riders*, a man "slipped a pistol from his pocket and stared at me for some minutes." The siege ended when local police arrived. The officers escorted the bus to the edge of the city.

An Alabama highway patrol officer tries to ease tensions in Anniston. After the firebombing, Riders were taken to a hospital. Many felt sick from inhaling smoke.

The Explosion

As the Greyhound bus left Anniston, segregationists followed it in their cars. Six miles later, the bus stalled with flat tires, which had been slashed. Once again, the mob went on the attack. For at least twenty minutes, they rocked and pounded on the bus. One person smashed a window. Then it happened: Cecil "Goober" Llewallyn threw a bundle of flaming rags into the bus.

"Burn them alive!" one of the segregationists shouted. Some white men leaned against the door so that the Riders could not escape. These men ran away only after the bus's fuel tank exploded. At that point, most Riders ran out the door. Others climbed out a window and landed hard on the ground. Finally, highway patrol officers arrived and dispersed the mob.

Why were the segregationists so angry with the Freedom Riders? Because they considered them "outside agitators"— meaning civil rights activists from the North. The segregationists resented that they would come into the South and try to change their way of life.

However, the Freedom Riders were just as determined to achieve equality for southern African Americans. Said Hank Thomas, as recounted in the book *On the Road to Freedom*: "I was hit over the head with a club. Even now my chest hurts and I almost conk out every time I climb a few steps. But I'm ready to volunteer for another ride. Sure. Any time."

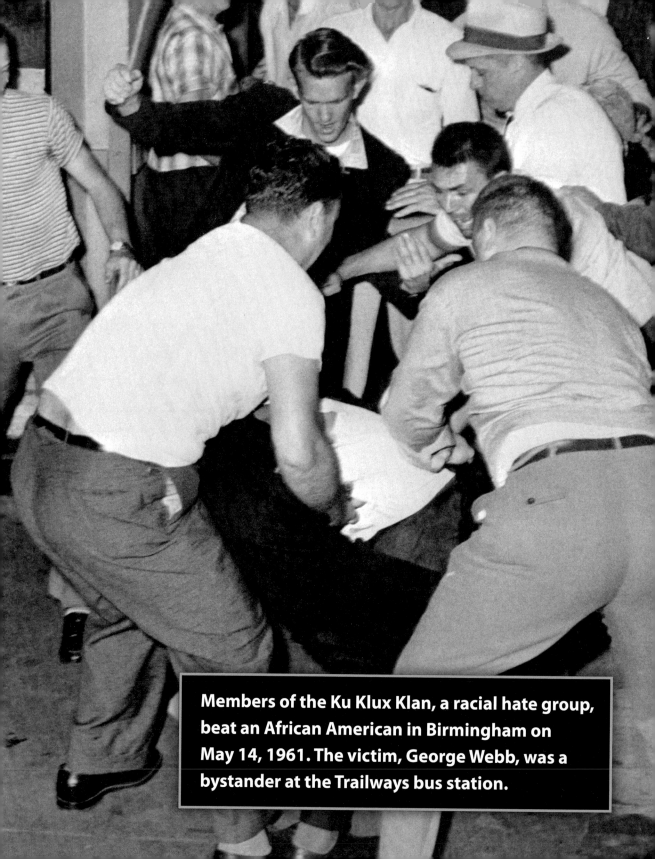

Members of the Ku Klux Klan, a racial hate group, beat an African American in Birmingham on May 14, 1961. The victim, George Webb, was a bystander at the Trailways bus station.

Chapter 2

Battered in
BIRMINGHAM

Beaten on the Bus

Like the Greyhound bus, the Trailways bus also pulled into Anniston on May 14. Eight white men forced their way onto the bus. They ordered the driver to continue to Birmingham. On the way, the men forcibly "segregated" the bus: They dragged black Freedom Riders to the back of the bus. They also beat white Freedom Riders. "I didn't get it so bad," white Freedom Rider James Peck said in *Voices of Freedom*, "but [Walter] Bergman got it so bad that he later had a stroke and has been paralyzed ever since."

Angry whites attacked Freedom Rider James Peck (pictured) on the bus ride from Anniston to Birmingham. He was abused again once he departed the bus. Howard K. Smith of CBS Radio said that Peck's "face was beaten and kicked until it was a bloody pulp."

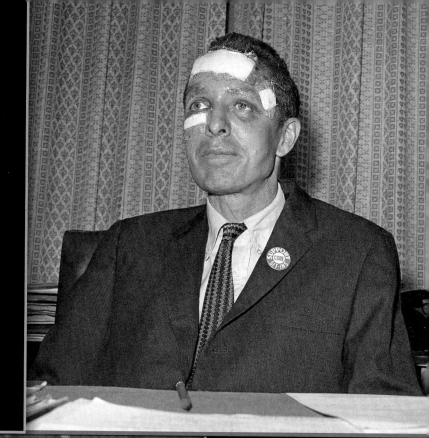

Birmingham public safety commissioner Eugene "Bull" Connor was a well-known segregationist. He knew that a white mob would greet the Freedom Riders in Birmingham. But he didn't send police there, he said, because it was Mother's Day.

Pounded With Pipes

Birmingham, Alabama, was one of the South's most fiercely segregated cities. When the Trailways bus pulled into Birmingham on May 14, about twenty whites aimed to teach the Freedom Riders "a lesson."

While waiting for the bus to arrive, the mob members carried clubs and metal pipes. Birmingham public safety commissioner Eugene "Bull" Connor decided not to send police. He *wanted* the segregationists to attack the Freedom Riders. And they did. Howard K. Smith of CBS Radio reported: "Toughs grabbed the passengers into alleys and corridors, pounding them with pipes, with key rings, and with fists."

Freedom Rider Walter Bergman, who was sixty years old, had been beaten badly on the bus. Once in Birmingham, he was kicked repeatedly in the head. He suffered brain damage. James Peck had his teeth kicked in. The cuts on his face required fifty-three stitches. After fifteen minutes of assaults, the police arrived. Some of the abused Freedom Riders went to the hospital. Others stayed at the home of the Reverend Fred Shuttlesworth, a black civil rights leader in Birmingham.

With their attacks in Anniston and Birmingham, segregationists had seemingly ended the Freedom Rides. But they didn't. Young activists in Nashville, Tennessee, wanted to start a new Freedom Ride.

A Fresh Group of Riders

On May 17, ten members of the Nashville Student Movement arrived in Birmingham. They were determined to start another Freedom Ride. The leader of this group, Diane Nash, explained their reasoning: "If the Freedom Riders had been stopped as a result of violence, I strongly felt that the future of the [civil] rights movement was going to be cut short."

Reverend Fred Shuttlesworth (pointing) talks with Nashville students in Birmingham. He likely explained to them the dangers they would face as Freedom Riders. As a civil rights leader, Shuttlesworth had faced several violent attacks in Birmingham. On Christmas Day, 1956, his house was bombed while he slept.

Connor Says "Go Away"

The Nashville students had the support of Robert Kennedy. He was the U.S. attorney general and the brother of President John F. Kennedy. Robert convinced the Greyhound Company to allow the Nashville Freedom Riders on another bus. However, Bull Connor was not so welcoming. When the Nashville students arrived in Birmingham to begin their Freedom Ride, he had them thrown in jail. The next day, police drove them back to Tennessee. The officers told the Riders not to come back to Alabama. But they did.

Freedom Riders John Lewis (left) and James Zwerg were beaten and bloodied by segregationists in Montgomery, Alabama. In this photo, Zwerg is removing teeth from his mouth.

Chapter 3

Trouble in
MONTGOMERY

Left to a Hostile Mob

On May 20, the Nashville Freedom Riders returned to Alabama, this time to Montgomery. Along the way, Alabama state police cars escorted their bus. But when the bus arrived in Montgomery, the police drove away. As the young Riders exited the bus, a hostile crowd of about three hundred whites waited for them. "They started beating everyone," recalled Freedom Rider Ruby Doris Smith in the book *Soon We Will Not Cry*. "I saw John Lewis beaten, blood coming out of his mouth. . . . Every one of the fellows was hit." Newspapers reported the event all over the world.

On the night of May 21, rioting erupted outside Montgomery's First Baptist Church. Segregationists set cars on fire. This car was flipped over.

Frightening events occurred at the First Baptist Church on May 21. A large mob surrounded the church. Hundreds of African Americans were trapped inside.

Trapped in the Church

Freedom Riders took a terrible beating at the Montgomery bus station on May 20. However, they refused to back down. The next night, they gathered at the First Baptist Church in Montgomery. More than 1,000 supporters, including Martin Luther King, Jr., joined them. U.S. attorney general Robert Kennedy feared for the safety of the Freedom Riders and their supporters. He sent six hundred federal marshals to Montgomery to protect them.

The marshals were not enough. That night, a mob of about 3,000 whites surrounded the church. They threw stones through the windows and set cars on fire. The marshals were outnumbered. When they tried to disperse the crowd by unleashing tear gas, it only made things worse. The tear gas wafted into the church. African Americans coughed and rubbed their burning eyes.

At 3 A.M., King phoned Robert Kennedy, pleading for help. King said that police or soldiers were needed to send the mob away. "If they don't get here immediately, we're going to have a bloody confrontation," King said, as recounted in the book *Parting the Waters*. "Because they're at the door now."

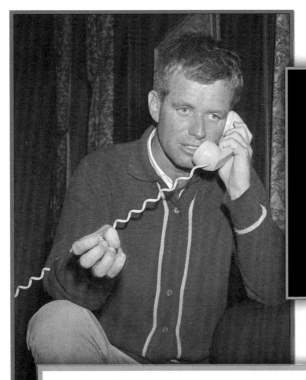

U.S. attorney general Robert Kennedy talks on the phone to Alabama governor John Patterson on May 21. Kennedy demanded that Patterson help the African Americans trapped inside the First Baptist Church.

Troops Disperse the Mob

Alabama governor John Patterson, a segregationist, did not like the Freedom Riders. Nevertheless, he agreed to rescue them. He sent state police and the Alabama National Guard to the First Baptist Church. The troops dispersed the mob and escorted African Americans out of the church.

President John F. Kennedy was frustrated with the Freedom Riders. He thought they were causing too much trouble and inciting too much violence. But the Freedom Riders were achieving their goals. Millions of Americans supported their efforts and demanded an end to segregation.

More Volunteer to Ride

On May 22, all eyes were on Montgomery, Alabama. A thousand National Guardsmen patrolled the city. In addition, more young activists drove to Montgomery. They volunteered to continue the Freedom Rides. Some came from CORE. Others were college-age civil rights activists from SNCC (Student Nonviolent Coordinating Committee). They were determined to ride a Freedom bus to Mississippi—a state as hostile to civil rights "agitators" as Alabama.

National Guard troops would protect Freedom Riders when they ventured into Mississippi.

Chapter 4

The Journey to
MISSISSIPPI

"Willing to Face Death"

On May 23, 1961, Martin Luther King, Jr., announced that the Freedom Rides would continue. A dozen Riders would leave the next morning on a bus from Montgomery to Jackson, Mississippi. Most white residents of that state staunchly opposed integration. King feared the worst. "Freedom Riders must develop the quiet courage of dying for a cause . . . " he told reporters. "I'm sure these students are willing to face death if necessary." Sixteen reporters and a dozen National Guard soldiers accompanied the Freedom Riders. No other passengers were on the bus.

On May 23 in Montgomery, civil rights leaders announce that the Freedom Rides will continue. John Lewis speaks into the microphone, sitting next to (left to right) James Farmer, Ralph Abernathy, and Martin Luther King, Jr.

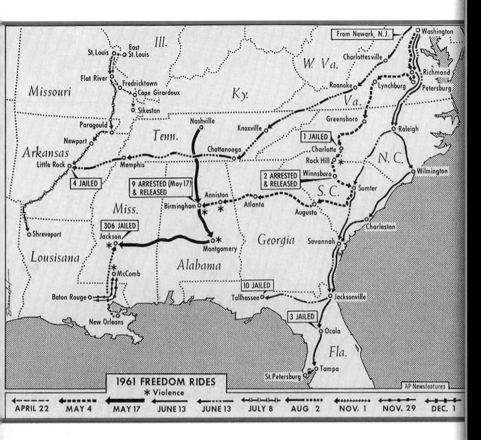

The Bus to Jackson

On May 24, Robert Kennedy felt comfortable that no violence would occur on the Montgomery-to-Jackson Freedom Ride. National Guardsmen were on the bus. Escorting the bus were police cars, helicopters, and U.S. Border Patrol airplanes. Officials in Mississippi agreed that the Riders would not be harmed. However, they also said that the Riders would be arrested once they arrived in Jackson.

The Second Bus

On the morning of May 24, a second group of Freedom Riders emerged. More than a dozen civil rights activists purchased Greyhound bus tickets from Montgomery to Jackson. Hank Thomas was one member of this Freedom Rider group. He had been on the burning bus in Anniston. As this bus was ready to leave, National Guardsmen climbed aboard. They accompanied the Riders on this second bus to Jackson.

This is one of the two Freedom Rides buses that traveled from Montgomery to Jackson. It was announced that the first bus would drive nonstop, with no bathroom breaks, for 250 miles.

Freedom Riders Julia Aaron (left) and David Dennis look stressed during their Montgomery-to-Jackson Freedom Ride. The National Guard soldiers protected them during the ride. But once they arrived in Jackson, they were at the mercy of local law officers. In reality, the soldiers had little to do on the bus. None of the passengers were "enemies." They were just Freedom Riders and reporters.

The second busload of Freedom Riders arrived at the Jackson bus station on May 24. They were immediately arrested. Here, the fifteen Riders on that bus are loaded into a police paddy wagon.

Chapter 5

Hundreds Sent to PRISON

Jailed in Jackson

On May 24, the two Freedom Rides buses pulled into Jackson. At the bus terminal, no mobs awaited them. However, many police officers were on hand. When the black Freedom Riders entered the whites-only waiting room, officers arrested all the Riders, black and white, on both buses. Their crime was violating Mississippi's segregation law. Two days later, all twenty-seven Riders went on trial. They did not stand a chance in the southern courtroom. When the Riders' lawyer spoke, the judge turned his back on him. The judge sentenced the Freedom Riders to sixty days in jail.

Sent to the Prison Farm

At first, the Freedom Riders were jailed in two different places. At the county jail, "we were met by some of the meanest looking tobacco-chewing lawmen I have ever seen," Freedom Rider Frank Holloway said in the book *Freedom's Main Line*. The Riders irritated the guards by singing freedom songs. "Oh-h, come on up to the fronta the bus/I'll be riding up there," they sang. At one point, Riders were transferred to the Hinds County prison farm. Conditions there were worse. When Freedom Rider C. T. Vivian refused to address a guard as "sir," the guard bashed his head.

Freedom Rider John Lewis enters a police van after his arrest in Jackson. He still wears a bandage over a wound from a previous attack.

Riders Pour Into Jackson

The Freedom Riders became heroes to justice-seekers across the land. Soon after the twenty-seven Riders were arrested, more Riders went to Jackson. By early June, dozens arrived and were arrested. Altogether that summer, more than three hundred Freedom Riders were jailed in Jackson.

These Freedom Riders left New Orleans on May 30, 1961. Their destination was Jackson, where they knew they would be arrested and jailed.

Abused in Prison

The spirit of the Freedom Rides became contagious. In the summer of 1961, more than four hundred activists participated in more than sixty Freedom Rides. They started or ended in Tennessee, Georgia, Louisiana, Missouri, Texas, and other states. Many whites rode the buses for justice, including priests and rabbis. Norma Wagner did, too. She was a blind white woman.

In Mississippi, many Freedom Riders were sent to Parchman Penitentiary. Guards often treated those prisoners terribly. When Riders refused to stop singing freedom songs, guards took away their mattresses and removed the screens from their windows. Mosquitoes swarmed their cells. To keep the bugs from biting, guards sprayed the prisoners with DDT—a harmful chemical.

In other jails, many Freedom Riders were badly beaten. In *Civil Rights Chronicle*, white Rider Ralph Fertig recalled that attackers "crushed my every rib." While leaving jail, Fertig asked a group of black Southerners, "How do you keep from hating white folks?"

Chapter 6

Freedom Riders PREVAIL

Hailed as Heroes

By the summer of 1961, many Americans viewed the Freedom Riders as warriors and heroes. Thousands of African Americans worked for civil rights in the South. But to black citizens in the South, the Freedom Riders were considered special. Wrote Juan Williams in *Eyes on the Prize*: "Civil rights workers . . . would be asked by local blacks, 'Are you one of them Freedom Riders?' . . . The courage and tenacity of those pioneers had captured the imagination and awe of blacks throughout the Southland." The Freedom Rides continued until the fall of 1961. They ended in victory.

President John F. Kennedy meets with civil rights activists in July 1961. Kennedy did not like the Freedom Rides because of the violence involved. However, he believed that African Americans were entitled to equal rights. He tried to help their cause. In 1963, he urged Congress to pass a civil rights bill to end racial segregation.

The Signs Come Down

On July 19, 1961, President John F. Kennedy announced his support of the Freedom Riders. He said that anyone who traveled across the country "should be able to do so freely." They should sit where they wanted to on buses. "Colored only" restrooms and waiting rooms, he believed, should be abolished.

Robert Kennedy urged the Interstate Commerce Commission (ICC) to take strong action. On September 22, 1961, the ICC banned segregation at interstate highway facilities. The ban went into effect on November 1. By that day, most bus-terminal officials had followed that order. They took down "colored" and "white" signs. Restrooms, waiting rooms, and restaurants were now open to everyone.

Thus, the Freedom Riders had achieved their goal. But civil rights activists had more battles to fight. In the South, most African Americans still could not vote. They were not hired for good-paying jobs. Their schools were subpar. In short, they were still treated like second-class citizens.

Civil rights leaders, including Martin Luther King, Jr., tried to build on the Freedom Rides' success. Throughout the 1960s, they staged hundreds of protests. They marched. They went to jail. They sang freedom songs. Their most famous song, "We Shall Overcome," reflected their determination.

SCENICRUISE

Freedom Riders from New York arrive in Jackson on August 14. They were likely among the three hundred Freedom Riders arrested in that city in 1961.

CORE members Jerome Smith (left) and Ed Blankenheim (right) share a bus ride together. When Smith was a child, he had sat in the white section of a bus. This impressed an elderly black woman. When Smith and the woman got off the bus, she told him, "Never stop doing what you're doing."

U.S. Congressman John Lewis receives a 2010 Presidential Medal of Freedom from President Barack Obama. An origina Freedom Rider, Lewis helped lead marches in Selma, Alabama. He also delivered a fiery speech at the March on Washington, an important civil rights event.

The 2011 Student Freedom Ride

Fifty years after the Freedom Rides, the Student Freedom Riders journeyed through the South. Their voyage coincided with the documentary *Freedom Riders*, which aired on *PBS* in 2011. The forty college students were of various ethnic backgrounds and came from all over the country. They rode on a bus that retraced the route of the original Freedom Rides. From May 6 to 16, 2011, they traveled from Washington, D.C., to New Orleans, Louisiana. They stopped in eighteen cities and met with original Freedom Riders.

Tariq Meyers, one of these Student Freedom Riders, met an elderly African-American woman in New Orleans. She had grown up in the segregated South. Seeing the new Freedom Riders flooded her with emotion. "Tears running down her face, she thanked me," Meyers wrote on the *PBS* website *Freedom Writers*, "thanked me for caring."

The woman had seen discrimination in the South much of her life. Even in recent years, African Americans have struggled more than others to overcome obstacles. On average, black citizens still make lower wages than whites. A black male is seven times more likely to go to prison than a white man.

The woman looked Meyers in the eyes. She said it was up to him to fight for freedom and racial equality. "It's your turn now," she said. "Don't let nothing turn you around."

Conclusion

The last known Freedom Ride occurred on December 10, 1961. That day, an African-American teenager named Joan Browning rode a segregated bus to Albany, Georgia. Albany, it turned out, would be the site of the next great civil rights battle.

Martin Luther King, Jr., and others led several large civil rights campaigns in the 1960s. Battlegrounds included Albany (1961–1962), Birmingham, Alabama (1963), Mississippi (1964), and Selma, Alabama (1965).

The locals pronounced Albany as *Al-benny*. In 1961, it remained a strongly segregated city. Thousands of African Americans attempted to change that. These Albany activists staged sit-ins at whites-only stores. They went on marches with signs that read "Freedom in Albany Now!" and "Don't Hinder Me." They sang freedom songs, such as "We Shall Overcome." In the first two weeks of the campaign, Albany police arrested nearly five hundred protesters.

King and other civil rights leaders hoped that the Albany movement would garner national publicity. It did but not very much. Albany police chief Laurie Pritchett made sure that the arrests were orderly and peaceful. If officers had beaten African Americans with clubs, it would have been shown on national TV news shows. Americans would have been outraged. They would have demanded that Congress and the president put an end to segregation in the South. Pritchett successfully kept the peace in Albany. No outrage was sparked.

The 1963 Birmingham campaign, however, was a different story. Public Safety Commissioner Bull Connor was known as a hothead. When thousands of African Americans protested segregation in his city, he went on the attack. He ordered firefighters to open their fire hoses on marchers. The force of the water was strong enough to break a person's ribs. Connor also ordered police officers to unleash their attack dogs. "I want to see the dogs work!" Connor declared.

Americans saw these images on the TV news, and they were appalled. So, too, was President John F. Kennedy. He urged Congress to pass a strong civil rights bill, one that would make segregation illegal.

In August 1963, seventy-four-year-old civil rights leader A. Philip Randolph led the March on Washington for Jobs and Freedom. That is where King delivered his famous "I Have a Dream" speech. A quarter-million people attended the march. Most were African American, but many white supporters attended, too. The message was clear: Most Americans wanted an end to segregation in the South.

The nation mourned President Kennedy's assassination on November 22, 1963. However, President Lyndon Johnson continued Kennedy's work for a civil rights bill. President Johnson urged Congress to pass the Civil Rights Act of 1964. He was successful. The act banned segregation in public places throughout the United States. It also gave the U.S. government more power to enforce anti-segregation laws.

The next year, Congress passed the Voting Rights Act of 1965. Together, these two acts largely (though not entirely) ended segregation in the South. Signs that read "Colored Entrance" and "Whites Only" were torn down. African Americans began to vote in large numbers. In future years, they would elect black politicians who addressed the concerns of black citizens. In 2008, Americans would even elect the first black president: Barack Obama.

The Freedom Riders did not ride just for their own freedom. They rode for the freedom of black Americans of their day and future generations. Take the case of Freedom Rider David Dennis, who was arrested in a whites-only waiting area in Louisiana. That arrest occurred on August 4, 1961—the very same day that President Obama was born.

1865–1965: After slavery, African Americans in the South are confined to segregated (separate, inferior) facilities. They are denied other citizenship rights, such as voting.

1954: The U.S. Supreme Court bans segregation in public schools.

1955–1956: Martin Luther King, Jr., leads a successful yearlong boycott of segregated buses in Montgomery, Alabama.

1957: The National Guard helps black students integrate Central High School in Little Rock, Arkansas.

1960–mid-1960s: Civil rights activists stage hundreds of sit-ins at segregated restaurants, stores, theaters, libraries, and many other establishments.

1961: Activists stage Freedom Rides on segregated buses in the South.

1963: Thousands of African Americans protest segregation in Birmingham, Alabama.

1963: A quarter-million Americans attend the March on Washington for Jobs and Freedom in Washington, D.C.

1964: Activists register black voters in Mississippi during "Freedom Summer."

1964: The U.S. Congress passes the Civil Rights Act. It outlaws segregation and other racial injustices.

1965: African Americans protest voting injustice in Selma, Alabama.

1965: Congress passes the Voting Rights Act, which guarantees voting rights for all Americans.

Further Reading

Books

Anderson, Dale. *Freedom Rides: Campaign for Equality.* Mankato, Minn.: Compass Point Books, 2008.

Bausum, Ann. *Freedom Riders: John Lewis and Jim Zwerg on the Front Lines of the Civil Rights Movement.* Washington: National Geographic Children's Books, 2005.

McWhorter, Diane. *A Dream of Freedom.* New York: Scholastic, 2004.

Sharp, Anne Wallace. *The Freedom Rides.* Detroit: Lucent Books, 2012.

Internet Addresses

Freedom Riders
<http://www.pbs.org/wgbh/americanexperience/freedomriders/>

The Freedom Riders, Then and Now
<http://www.smithsonianmag.com/history-archaeology/The-Freedom-Riders.html>

Index